EXPLORATIONS

EXPLORATIONS

Poems by Dick Greene

Antrim House

Simbsury, Connecticut

Library of Congress Control Number: 2009940205

ISBN: 978-0-9823970-5-3

Printed & bound by Sterling Pierce Co., Inc.

First Edition, 2009

Cover photograph by Kent Miles, "English Gardens, 1981"
copyright © 1981 by Kent Miles (www.kentmiles.com)

Photograph of author by Celeste Greene

Book Design by Rennie McQuilkin

Antrim House
860.217.0023
AntrimHouse@comcast.net
www.AntrimHouseBooks.com
21 Goodrich Road, Simsbury, CT 06070

To my wife, Celeste, who inspired several of the poems in this book, encourages me in my poetry even when it takes time from more practical chores, is my most fruitful source of editorial advice, and laughs at my jokes.

SPECIAL THANKS

This is to acknowledge the many and diverse readers of my emailed Poem of the Week, who have provided me with feedback and encouragement. Their spontaneous expressions of appreciation are a reassuring vote of confidence and their candid comments and suggestions particularly helpful. Every Sunday, when my Poem of the Week is mailed, I look forward to the ensuing exchange of reflections on life and poetry. Thank you, readers, for the many pleasurable Sundays you've given me and for the inspiration your responses have provided for my writing.

I'd also like to express my appreciation to my editor and publisher, Rennie McQuilkin, who did a masterful job in designing this book and, above all, in helping me organize its contents.

TABLE OF CONTENTS

THE WORLD WE LIVE IN

DARK MATTER

STILL DELIGHTING

We shall not cease from exploration
And the end of all our exploring
Will be to arrive where we started
And know the place for the first time.

T. S. Eliot, *Four Quartets,* "Litle Gidding"

PROLOGUE

BECOMING T. S. ELIOT

When I was young and impressionable
I wanted to be T. S. Eliot.
No matter that I didn't understand much of his poetry.
I felt a man of letters was the most admirable thing to be.
As for the physical heroes of yore,
I knew that wasn't me,
and having been "poet laureate" of my eighth grade class,
I aspired to emulate
that paragon of modernity.
The first step I took
was to get horn-rimmed glasses
though I hardly needed glasses yet.
I wear glasses still
but, as far as I can tell,
they did nothing for my poetry.

LIFE AND DEATH

Of those prime themes of poetry,
love and death,
I'm not much interested in the latter.
Perhaps I lack eschatological fervor,
am more interested in beginnings
and prefer the ebb and flow of events
to the place where they fall off the edge.

Not that the theme lacks power.
Maybe it's that we can do nothing about it,
and I'm more interested in those destinies
we can temper.
Of death let other poets write.
I'll explore life.

EARLY YEARS

In the Beginning

I was there
when you were squeezed
from your mother's womb,
coming into the world
not like a deity,
clean, calm and complete,
but as a man does,
red, wrinkled and vulnerable,
looking bewildered and indignant,
like a turtle deprived of its shell.

THE BEAR

I found a worn teddy bear in our attic,
one half-remembered
as if only a dream.
When I squeezed it
it played a lullaby,
a tune I remembered
without knowing its source,
and with that tune came back
a time before memory,
a time I knew only from photographs:
of my mother
younger than I could recall
smiling with pleasure at me,
of myself still bald and stubby-legged
or lofted gleefully on a teeter-totter
or a bit later
posed and pensive
with a halo of light brown curls.

For years that bear
lay in its box
waiting for me to pick it up,
that bear I can no longer find.

West Side Memories

We lived across from the planetarium,
mere yards from the sky,
while just down the street
was the el,
and still vivid
under the long gone girders,
a barbershop
with its candy stripe pole
and its carousel pony
astride which young clients sat,
at the center of the universe.

First Tug

"I've got a fish," I shouted.
I was five,
gone fishing with my father
in his boat with oars I tried
but couldn't manage.
It seemed such a long time I sat there
dangling a worm in the water,
the boat gently rocking
in the drowsy summer sunshine,
when suddenly there was a tug on my line,
that first tug
of a lifetime.

THE CLIMBING TREE

The tree was tall
but made for climbing,
branches close to the ground,
thick foliage
where we could perch
concealed from the world
like secret birds,
branches closely spaced,
a Jacob's ladder
into the airy realm
of birds and squirrels
and the daydreams
of tree climbers.

THE KITE

The kite
dances on air
still joined to our hand
capering to our command
as if its string
were an extension
of our nerves.
Through it we reach
cloud high
as if we rode the wind
and the whole wide sky
blew through our hair.

SUMMER IS HERE NOW

Summer is here now
as I remember it
consecrated by fireworks:
the long languorous days
tedious sometimes
but still sweet;
swimming in the lake
where skin and cool water meet
and fish dart away
from this alien invader;
water slapping on boat or dock
or weaving nets of sunlight on a boathouse wall;
the white froth of bow cleaving wave;
a sail flapping lazily as we come about;
or in a rowboat
suspended between water and sky
waiting for fish to bite;
playing into the dark hours;
and through the night
the myriad sounds of insects
and the lullaby of frogs.

At the Beach

Summers at the beach
we turned pink on the yellow sand,
wore grit like a second skin,
fast high-stepped to the water
on sand sometimes so hot
we tried to run without touching ground,
splashed into the cooling water,
tasting its brine,
our nostrils full of that scent
that told us where we were
when we first drew near the shore,
swam out to waves
that carried us headlong on their crests,
whirling us down as they crumbled,
supplying us with breathless tales
when we were back on land.
Then we walked on the wet sand
where water followed in our footprints
while we gathered shells and sand dollars
and flat, smooth stones
rounded by the tireless work of water,
and watched white-vested gulls,
those dapper beachcombers,
waddle down the strand
or, balancing on a breeze,
glide down the shore
like notes of an arpeggio.

Then late in the day
when we were tired and the tide came in,

mesmerized by the ocean's pulse
we watched it rise on the beach,
dissolving sand castles
so painstakingly wrought,
then, nonchalantly, slide back down,
and at night
the timeless sound of breaking waves
lulled us to sleep.

PULLMAN MEMORIES

Riding a train
takes me back
to those boyhood summers
when I traveled alone
from New York to Chicago,
starting from Grand Central Station
with a gentle jolt,
gathering momentum
past the vacant-eyed apartments
of upper Manhattan,
wondering about the people
who lived inside,
then over to the river
where we hit full stride,
our wheels clicking
at a Dixieland pace,
the Hudson Valley scrolling by,
lake-wide river, stubs of old mountain,
the play of light in a cloud-crowded sky,
until we turned off at Albany
into mile on mile of farms and woods,
imagining myself again
into the houses
along the right of way,
those who might live within
seeming not quite real,
as we no doubt to them,
two worlds
sliding by one another

each in its own continuum
of time and space.

Then in the dining car,
self-conscious but proud,
the center of attention
in that adult place,
and not long after
in my berth,
snug as a tent,
shaken down to sleep
by the jiggling of the train,
waking during the night
when we stopped
at some anonymous station,
pulling the window shade up a crack
to see if I could make out a sign
of where we were,
watching the moving figures
swathed in steam,
silhouetted against the platform lights.

Then it was morning
and the flat fields of Indiana
were wheeling by,
telephone poles
riffling by
at a dizzy pace.
Like a horse

galloping back to its stable
we seemed to accelerate
as we drew near our destination.
I felt I had to hurry getting dressed
lest I would still be in my pajamas
when we reached Dearborn Station
where the train might be shunted off
before I emerged,
my father on the platform muttering,
"Where is that boy?"
But we slowed down
as we swam into the denser landscape
and instead of being caught unprepared
I waited impatiently
for that endless city
to end.

RIVERWORLD

Where the small Midwestern river
issued from its lake,
running smooth and brown
under a translucent vault of willows,
I went exploring
when I was ten or so,
imagining myself a voyageur
descending the mighty Mississippi.

There I encountered exotic fauna,
catfish with their mandarin whiskers,
looking learned and wise,
mud-puppies emerging from the water
like the first sea creatures
venturing onto land.
There sandy banks
sank into sepia waters
and a sunlit world
was steeped in mystery.

Dad

When I was small
and we'd leave some relative's house
where we'd been visiting at night,
my father would carry me to the car
telling me about the stars
and I would ask
"What was there before the stars?"
Or he'd sing to me, and I'd say,
"Daddy, you sing like Bing Crosby."
But that was before I was embarrassed
by his telling everybody
how much our belongings cost,
and before he began to tell me
"You don't appreciate
how important money is."
We were separated forever
by that tectonic drift,
for he died
before I was capable of seeing his needs
through the glare of my disapproval.

WORLD'S FAIR

I went to my first world's fair
when I was eight.
As is the way with such events
it was more about us
than the world,
and refracted the future
through optimist eyes.
You wouldn't have known
from anything on display
that a cancer festered
in Europe's bosom
or that the most brutal of wars
was mere months away.
Nor was there any inkling
of the baleful new words
soon to be unleashed
on our vocabulary,
blitzkrieg, storm trooper, quisling,
kamikaze, Hiroshima,
holocaust,
while the Futurama
with its ebullient guides
depicted a morrow
of shining towers
where poverty was ostracized.
Oh, the world looked good
in our neighborhood
in the spring of '39.

SEPTEMBER 1, 1939

Where was I?
At home in our tranquil suburb?
In school, or was it too soon?
Playing with friends?
Reading in my room?
Still at the lake perhaps
or on a train
coming home.
I don't know what time of day it was,
don't think I even heard the news.
My parents surely knew
but they must have said
best not tell the children.
Nor did I know of Kristallnacht,
Munich,
the Sudetenland,
Anschluss.

It was probably summery still,
the leaves unchanged,
a calm September day.

Growing Up

While I was growing up in a comfortable suburb
a million and a half children,
Jews like myself,
died in camps
not like the ones where we passed our summers.
While I dallied down the tree-lined street to school
past big houses and spacious yards
those other children
were turned out of their schools and homes.
While I studied Hebrew and piano lackadaisically
those other children learned firsthand
the meaning of the Kaddish and the dirge.
While I pushed away the food
my grandmother urged on me
those other children grew thin
till they seemed not much more than skeletons.
And while I lay in my familiar bed
in my lovingly furnished room
fretting, perhaps, about a catch I'd flubbed,
but nonetheless falling asleep easily,
those other children slept fitfully
disturbed by barrack sounds
and nightmares of men in jackboots
and the smoke from chimneys.

UNDER THE APPLE BOUGHS

There was a wall along the road
where we played soldier
behind the loosely stacked stones.
Next to it a row of mountain birch,
tops tinted with evening sun.
Then the house
in dappled coat of whitewashed brick
and the orchard with gnarled trees
where we pressed apples on chill fall days
and savored the cold, sweet cider.

Outside my bedroom window
a magnolia tree glistened
and, beyond, a broad lawn
sloped down to the pond
where frogs held nightly congress
and I learned of mallards
and snapping turtles
and green-winged teals.
There we skated in winter
until darkness hid the agate surface
and swam impatiently in spring,
the ice barely melted,
as if our innocence protected us from cold.

Between pond and house
stood a lone apple tree
where, as I watched at first light,
pheasants gathered

in their courtly plumage
to feast on windfalls.

Then bombs fell on Pearl Harbor
and soldier games gave way to war.

EARLY EXPLORER

Living in L.A.
when it was much smaller than today
I ranged far
on my balloon-tire Schwinn
from our suburban fastness
eastward down the daylong boulevard
rolling the city's length,
like LaSalle
exploring the great mid-continental waterway,
past movie houses
and department stores
full of siren temptations,
past buildings monotonous as waves
toward the city's towered center
which I saw each time longingly from afar
but reached only once
having to turn back time and again
to be home before dark,

or westward toward the ocean,
that shore I never reached,
picturing its blue expanse
with dogged anticipation
as I toiled my way
past mile on mile
of urban Gobi,

or over the high hills to the north
through untamed canyons
with their boulder-strewn streams

and groves of scrub oak
to the range's far shoulders
overlooking a broad valley
that reached into the blue-gray distance
(imagining myself a pioneer surmounting
the last westward fold of the Sierra)
then down to the citrus groves
where I lingered
among multitudes of orange globes
in the welcoming shade.

PIE

Apple, blueberry, cherry, peach,
coconut custard, banana cream,
boyhood's soft-focus dreams.

I used to stop at the bakery
on the way home from school
to buy an individual pie,
one just the size for a boy
but an aunt with whom I stayed for a while
forbade me them,
deeming pies bad for one's health.
Seeing me once munching one
as I ambled home
she gave me a scolding so fierce
I flinch from it to this day
when pie is forbidden me again
under the strictures of age.

Shades of Simple Simon,
Tom Sawyer, Huckleberry Finn,
and maybe Adam too,
for what do you suppose was his favorite dish
after that first taste of sin?
Which leads me to a metaphysical question:
was pie designed for boys
or boys for pie?

PICTURES THEN AND NOW

Time was, unknown to most of the young today,
when we went to movies in palaces,
not like Versailles or Buckingham, to be sure,
but vast, dark chambers
where shifting light beams played on mote-filled air
like sunlight falling through clouds,
where we passed our Saturday afternoons and evenings
immersed in adolescent murmurings,
entranced by motley patterns on a screen
or necking in a place called the balcony
like courtiers in some ornate nook
surprised there by Watteau.

LISTENING TO FATS WALLER

Listening to Fats Waller,
I think
this was the music of my mother's youth.
She danced like a flapper, I suppose,
something it can be hard
to imagine one's mother doing,
but she showed me the Charleston
when I was in my teens.
We danced it the only way you can,
energetically,
mother and son,
between the sofa and the baby grand.

SEVENTEEN

That summer I worked at a camp
not far from the city
on the other side of the river.
One of the counselors, Didi—
Shirly Lutz, from Akron Ohio—
was a lithe, compact girl
with a sweet smell of sunlight about her,
and as she sat in the high lifeguard chair,
her smooth legs crossed,
the guys would crowd around
like stage door Johnnies
vying for attention.

Didi and I had the same night off
and we'd go into the city
down to the Village
and all night smoky jazz,
heading back to camp
not long before dawn,
taking the nearly empty subway
to the bridge.
The buses didn't run at that hour
so we'd walk the mile across,
solitary voices
high above the water,
the sun rising at our backs,
our shadows stretching out
long as the life before us.

THE CREW

A crew is out for early practice
caressing the morning air
with rapt strokes
cleaving the smooth water
with rhythmic thrusts
feeling no doubt
it's good to be young
and drowsily awake
stretched out on a long-limbed river
this fine spring morning.

DRIVING TO THE SUN

From Paris
to the Costa del Sol
we drove
in my dilapidated convertible
in the springtime of our lives
down a long, straight Roman road
tunneling through pines
on into Spain,
drifting through Madrid, Granada, Sevilla,
then to Málaga,
the top down,
Colette and Serge
perched on the seat backs
waving to the earthbound
as we sailed through small towns
on our way to the sky.

BLOSSOM TIME

I remember the Massif Central
about this time of year
almost fifty years ago,
that high ground
spattered with new leaves,
small orchards blossoming here and there
but mostly a sprinkling of green
fresh as the clear streams
with their thin sheets of ice.
Why that spring
out of nearly seventy?
Perhaps it was freedom,
for I was a young soldier then
on leave,
driving from Heidelberg to Provence.
Perhaps it was the solitude
after the enforced society of military life,
alone and free
driving down a country road in France,
the world just greening,
the streams still braced with ice.

THE WORLD WE LIVE IN

To the Source

I've lived near the river's end,
where its wide waters slide
into bay and ocean,
and watched ships ride the deep water.
Often I've dreamed
of tracing it to its source,
past the farthest reach of ocean vessels,
past stretches where the silken flow
is trimmed with frothy white
and you can see the mountains' bones
beneath the water,
climbing, ever climbing
through field and forest
at last to the place
in a watery meadow perhaps
or hidden under trees
where the great river is born,
issuing from the earth
in a stream so small
you could cup it in your hands.

MARBLEHEAD

Sun-spangled
sail-flecked
homespun bay,
cloud-bannered
beach-blazoned,
yes wine-dark too,

a fanfare of trumpets
and cellos,
the somber brilliance
of a northern sea.

SEEING WATER

Even now, in my sixty-seventh year,
I still experience a thrill
when rounding a curve
or topping a hill
I come upon a body of water,
whether festive blue
or sullen gray,
open to view
or half hidden by trees.
Even a small lake
I pass almost every day
still surprises me
with a pulse of pleasure.
It summons up, I suppose,
the lake where I spent
my childhood summers,
its mile-wide waters
abloom with sails,
where I fished
as day segued into night
and gold streaked
the sky's book of hours,

the remote Canadian lakes
where I basked in a solitude
broken only by the lonely cry of loons,
moose grazing in the shallows
or the occasional band of Cree
in their quiet canoes,
gathering wild rice,

and overhead at night
the sky-spanning, pulsating
polychrome curtain
of the aurora,

or the Hudson
where I whiled away my time
watching ships slide languorously by,
the slow kaleidoscope
of clouds and sky
over the Jersey bank,
or seagulls
gliding against
the towering Palisades
so steady on their wings
the world seemed to move
while they stood still,
and in the background always
the tremendous harp of the bridge
gracing the river's canyon
as it might the very gates of heaven.

Then there's the Pacific
which, more precocious than Balboa,
I first saw at age six,
having come from the East
with my grandmother
who, indulging me,
drove straight to the water,

not even stopping
at our new home.
It was overcast that day
and I was disappointed
that the great ocean
wasn't the least bit blue.
Still, it was the Pacific,
spreading all the way
from California to Cathay
with a leap
only the imagination could equal.

ODE TO AN ISLAND

My sister lives on a Caribbean isle,
little more than a dust mote on a map,
no realm of magic,
nor Ariel, nor Caliban
(though a touch of each),
no stage for grand drama,
merely the familiar theater of domesticity,

but birds flower there
and flowers take flight,
fish flash rainbows over the coral,
palm fronds sway to the wind
as if spellbound in dance,
and in the night
as you drift into sleep
you hear the waves upon the reef
intoning the ancient anthem of the sea.

ORINOCOS OF THE IMAGINATION

I've never been to the Orinoco
and have seen few photos of it,
but I feel I know its sinuous lengths,
winding between thick jungle walls,
flashing silver in the sun,
delicate waterfalls
threading from cloud-shrouded cliffs,
dense foliage
adorned with birds of kindergarten colors
and jaguars that merge into shadow,
the insistent music
of bird cry and monkey chatter,
dugouts and caimans
scoring its sleek waters,
those who people its valley
gliding nearly naked
through twilight forests,
dappled by the distant sun.
I know these lush landscapes
from my dreams.

COTOPAXI

Just below a great snowy cone in the Andes
on a broad flat shelf of mountain
wild horses race
keeping pace
with wind-driven clouds overhead
breath steaming
long manes swirling
exhilarated
as if created
just moments before
out of the primordial chaos.

A MANATEE COMES TO MANHATTAN

A manatee has been seen in the Hudson River
gawking at the tall buildings,
wondering at the absence
of mangroves and palm trees,
poking its W. C. Fields nose out of the water
as if it were about to don a top hat
and tap dance down Broadway.

This is just the beginning.
The climate's becoming warmer,
the seas are rising.
Soon manatees
will crowd our summer streets
like tourists with fanny packs.

Birds in Black

Stepping outside I find
mere feet from my door
two large crows
in a leafless tree.
Too large for its naked branches,
motionless,
with vitreous eyes,
they look like clockwork birds,
but in their gaze I see
wary minds
appraising me.

CROWS IN THE RAIN

I've always wondered what birds do in the rain.
Surprisingly, I've never seen.
Today I noticed a cluster of crows
hunched stoically (I imagined)
in a tree,
a cold November downpour
running down their backs.
One was clucking faintly
as if in misery.
Now I don't much care for crows
but seeing them pelted with icy water
gave me a shiver of sympathy
and I wanted them to be
somehow immune
to the wet and cold.
They must be, I thought,
or they wouldn't be sitting in a tree.
But then where would they sit,
those shifty, thieving,
suffering fellow creatures?

THE VOICES OF STONES

Who can look on Ayers Rock
without hearing songlines,
Stone Mountain
without Dixie or the Battle Hymn
ringing in one's inner ear,
Angkor or Machu Picchu
without phantom voices,
boulders without mountains' deep bass,
pebbles without the murmur of streams?
Who says that stones are mute?
They whisper, babble, boom, chant, sing.

POLISHED STONES

Beneath the leafy layers of the wood
folding green on green
the creek sings,
echoing the faint, discordant tones of reverie.

Under its sinuous surface
stones glimmer,
taking shape
like words.

Variations on a Year

1. First Notes

Though winter is with us still
the birds have begun to sing
to the cues of spring,
first a cardinal, then a wren
and now this morning in early March,
as a chill dawn pinks the sky,
the wistful fluting of a mourning dove
which, after winter's longueurs,
when few but crows were heard,
now finds itself bestirred
to loose its song.

2. What the March Wind Saw

blossoms and clouds blowing white
against a blue-washed sky

aureoles of daffodils
above the winter stubble

forsythia miming sunlight
amidst the leafless trees

budded boughs cascading
from early greening willows

birds, birds, undeterred
by all the bluster and chill

3. Spring Snow

Wet snow coats
twig, branch and bud.
Against the still black street
the waning season
limns its last words
in bold calligraphy.

4. Frabjous Day

The sky its brightest blue
the clouds their cleanest white
the air balmy
as young leaves
bedeck the trees
in their fairest green.
What a fine day to be on Earth
sailing around the sun.

5. Apple Factory

The apple tree
summoning its resources
like mother's milk
bears blossoms
and new young leaves.
Then the blossoms recede,
leaving fruit buds
and the leaves deploy their solar panels,
drawing from the air
the infinitesimal building blocks

of plants and anthracite and diamonds
to shape
red globes of fruit
shiny and sweet,
fashioned of earth and air and rain
and the fires of the sun.

6. Summer Morning

Night having gathered the haze
woven by the heat of day,
come dawn
has laid it to ground
adorning web and blade
with bright beads
while the sky,
stripped of its veils,
stuns with blue nakedness.

7. Summer's End

This morning
for the first time in months
it was cool enough
that I felt like wearing something
next to my skin.
All the summer's haze had gathered
into a few small clouds
hung out like newly washed sheets,
and migrant swans came down
on the wings of the wind.

8. Autumn Road

Autumn arrived with the wind today
on a highway of clouds
macadam grey
stretching flat bottomed
to the far horizon
through fields of flagrant blue.

9. Autumn Sonata

Sunlight pierces the clouds,
setting linden leaves aglow
yellow as daffodils
against a dove-gray, autumn sky,
as if the seasons were juxtaposed.
And I hear music playing
on a long ago gramophone,
the sound of strings
pressed between the years
like a blossom in the pages of a book.

10. It Was One of Those Fine October Days

It was one of those fine October days
free from summer's heat and haze
but not yet gripped by autumn chill.

It was one of those fine October days
when the sky's so clear
you can see the moon

through the atmosphere
at midday.

It was one of those fine October days
when the trees sport yellow and red
instead of their everyday summer green.

It was one of those fine October days
when one draws a deep breath
and is grateful
to be resident on Earth.

11. October Morning

The hazy morning air
though honey gold
supports no bees
only dry leaves
tracing their slow arabesques
toward the ground.

12. Geese on the Loose

Crowds of geese
over the lake
this fall fresh afternoon,
flying helter-skelter
not in neat formation
but in ragged troupes
honking raucously—
like partygoers

blowing away the old year,
tooting in the new—
joyously free, unbound by gravity,
nowhere they need to go
nothing they need to do.

13.   Chicago Winter

That winter the lake froze over,
ice piling up on the shore
like cards scattered
by a capricious hand.

I imagined what it would be like
walking to Michigan
sixty miles away on the far shore,
ice so wide
I would see the Earth's curve,
sun-bleached sky
blending into the frozen surface
in one vast, luminous chamber,
then stars stippling an infinity of night,
as if I had stepped out
into the universe.

VARIATIONS ON A DAY

1. Just Before Dawn

Pale green seeps
into the soft fabric of the night
as if dipped in light.
No stars in view,
their glitter subdued
by dawn's tide
and the moon's faint luminescence.
Only an appliqué of trees
adorns this dark tapestry.
That and a crescent moon.

2. Clouds

Over the high ridge
clouds blossom
from an emptiness
of flame-blue sky,
blossom and vanish
and blossom and vanish again
in a display
of planetary
prestidigitation.

3. Thundershower

The sunlight disappears
and looking up I see

the shining edge
of a large, dark cloud
sliding overhead
like an enormous ship.
I think I hear thunder
and soon the sound is distinct,
mingling with the exclamatory voices
of a family
on the path behind the trees.
Then large raindrops splatter
the deck beneath my feet
and I hear laughter
beyond the trees.

4.   The Lake at Evening

The sky is still,
the water too,
hushed,
expectant,
as the worldlight dims
and trees silhouette
a watery stage
where fish dimple
the plainsong surface
and birds pirouette
through the gilded air.

5.   Rowing

I like to row in evening
when dark trees

frame the still lake
and the water mirrors the sky,
to glide over the smooth surface,
stroking in slow rhythm,
leaning back on the oars,
sending spirals spinning
like galaxies
into the reflected sky.

6. Moon Madness

Stepping out our front door
I'm suddenly awash
in the cries of geese
filling every corner
of the night sky,
silhouettes bobbing
across the lunar disk,
a crowd of shadows
driven to mad dance
by the spectacle
of a full moon
floating free
of the planet's grasp.

DARK MATTER

MEMORIAL DAY

Hopewell, New Jersey, May 2005

It was enough to make us weep,
half a dozen veterans of the last great war
looking like fading away,
followed by the high school band
booming bravely into adulthood.
Next a squad in Civil War uniform
harking back to the source of the holiday,
a fratricide that seems today
to have occurred in another country,
not just another century.
Then a retired Humvee
with a small girl in back
wearing a grunt style cap
and waving mechanically;
vintage cars,
big ones from a century ago
with wooden spokes
and other vestiges of their carriage genes,
still boxy ones from the 20's,
the streamlined 30's,
the fishtailed 50's,
a couple of Mustangs, an early Corvette;
then the fire engines, big and bigger,
like armor-plated rhinos,
our town's brigade riding old fashioned red,
others yellow,
sage green from a well-heeled nearby town;
delegations of Boy Scouts, Cub Scouts, Brownies,

one scout troop with a five-piece band
trying like twenty-five;
a motorcycle club,
plenty of paunch and gray hair,
and, though some ponytails,
suburban angels rather than Hell's.
Finally a platoon of kids
all safely helmeted,
one tireless on a pogo stick,
others on scooters and bikes
and even a few on tricycles,
training for future wars.

THE THINGS THEY CARRY

I hear casually booming voices in the street
and, looking out the window, see
two boys in their early teens.
From the sound they might be men,
and I think of such almost-men
(still, I know, partly children)
some will grow up to be soldiers,
carry their childhood fantasies
into the world
like flags,
and I think
in another part of that world,
if not for good luck in where they were born,
these men-children would bear arms,
kill and be killed
before becoming men.
What could be more manly?

CITIZEN SOLDIER

I was a soldier once
in a far away land
though not on death's hallowed ground.
It was during an undeclared peace
and I went to an office every day
where I battled armies of paper,
and by night toiled in other ways
in beer halls and brothels.

There were field exercises, to be sure,
and Saturday parades
where we practiced maneuvers
unseen in warfare
since the redcoats were ambushed by the minutemen,
and our company commander polished
his patent leather holster
lovingly as an apple,
while we waited to march by
sharply aligned
as if all of one mind,
our bodies going one way
our minds another.

THE CHARMS OF WAR

It was a good war,
World War I,
for us Americans
who were in it only briefly
and didn't lose so many young men.
It had its compensations,
its mademoiselles,
its Hemingway,
old Europe
with its worldly charms,
and our heroically coming to its rescue.
Then tickertape parades
down lower Broadway,
and the best of times
in left bank cafés.
Would we have been there
if not for the war?

Then World War II
less romantic, true,
but righteous,
a war against evil,
the best of wars.
And even Nam,
food for nostalgia even there,
for we love war
and will, I suppose,
as long as men grow from boys.

Veterans Day 2006

Each day we read in the *Times*
the names of our soldiers
who've died in Iraq,
sometimes imagining bits of their lives,
the towns where they grew up,
their families,
their high school sweethearts,
their now grieving spouses and friends,
and we're saddened.
Yet more with the names of thousands,
mostly young men,
engraved in marble or granite,
their parents' hopes and dreams
interred in stone.
All that remains
a few keepsakes
and memories
of newborns, toddlers, vulnerable boys,
youths becoming men.

Who wanted those wars?
Their leaders of course,
but all too often those same young men,
and those who mourn for them.

In Memory Of

Another World War II pilot gone.
Obit on a back page of the *Times:*
"Pilot who downed Yamamoto dies at 84."
A photo of three lean young men in khakis
looking as if they never could be 80
posed in front of a fighter plane,
Pacific palms in the background.
He began high school about the time I was born
and I began it the year he downed the infamous admiral.
My cousin Bob was a fighter pilot in that war,
so much a part of my adolescent imagination,
and it's almost as if the young man in the photo,
now, unbelievably, deceased,
were my kin.
Obit the same day for Percy Goring, 106,
last British survivor of Gallipoli.
When I was a boy it was the last veteran of the Civil War
and, when a young man, the Spanish American.
For earlier generations it was the Revolutionary
the Hundred Years, the Punic, the Persian,
always one within reach of living memory,
and always some last veteran
to nurture
nostalgia for old wars.

Boots on the Ground

Put boots on the ground, they said,
as if they were dragons' teeth
which, sown, sprout spectral armies
that fade away, once battle is done,
leaving no blood behind.

They said nothing about
the men and boys
who would no longer have feet
to wear those boots,
or would wear them to their graves.

Remembering Vientiane

Known among early European visitors
for their gentleness and insouciance,
they lingered in a backwater
of this turbulent century.

I lived in their capital
near the broad Mekong
on a dirt lane
bracketed by old wooden temples,
unpainted and weather stained,
with their muffled bells
and slow traffic of orange-robed monks.

Only roosters
disturbed the peace,
until tanks came
clogging the narrow streets,
grinding them under ridged treads,
spewing manic metal
onto roofs and shutters,
like the rhetoric
of clashing ideologies,
and bodies erupted
from the river's smooth surface.

THE VETERANS

Of all the young men
who went to war
over half a century ago
still believing
in everlasting love
and life too long to think about,
confident they would return,
though only some did,
and confident they would get ahead,
though only some did,
many have fallen
from the ranks.

Of those who remain,
the hard muscles
that propelled them
across the fields of death,
and life,
have shrunk,
and their muscular ambitions
have withered.
Now they look back
and remember those days
when they went to war
fit and trim
and felt they could outrun mortality.

I See Myself Becoming Old

My closet is full of suits I don't wear anymore.
Nothing I need to wear them for.
There are days when I stay in my pajamas till noon.
I picture my heirs looking at my wardrobe one day
asking "Can you think of anyone who can use these
or should we give them to Goodwill?"
Or "Would you like this tie as a remembrance of Dad?"
As I read the obits of the recently deceased,
which I took to doing a few years ago,
I compare their ages to mine.

Then there's the arthritis in my hands and feet.
My left foot aches when I walk
and I suffered a rupture in a time-worn tendon not long ago.
I have more trouble lifting things and getting around.
Don't jump over puddles anymore
for fear of the damage I might do coming down.
(No more kicking up heels for me.)

What will it be next,
the incipient cataracts?
My hearing isn't what it used to be.
I don't think I need a hearing aid yet,
though my daughter disagrees.
Or will it be something unforeseen
like that ill-fated tendon?

I see myself becoming old,
yet it's as if I were watching it happen to somebody else.

On the Downhill Side

April's over
having, it seems, only just begun.
Once past the apex
we speed ever faster.
Ascending was slower.
The landscape labored by.
Each time you rounded a curve
there was another just ahead
and you never saw the summit
much less the decline on the other side.
Then one day you notice you're on the downgrade.
The landscape unreels
at an accelerating pace.
You glimpse lowlands in the distance
from time to time
but the road,
absorbed in its curves,
never reveals its destination.
Down you go,
wind pressed to your face,
applying the brakes
which no longer work the way they used to
and the last thing on your mind
is to shout whoopee.

MISOGYNISTIC MUTTERINGS

Remember those pubescent girls
who screamed for Frankie or Elvis,
hands pressed to cheeks,
mouths agape with ecstasy?
It's hard for me to imagine
what sort of carnal thrill
could have caused so much delirium
among maidens touched by no more
than the sight of a pompadoured youth
switching his hips in syncopation
or a skinny one
clutching a microphone,
as if it were a piece of anatomy.

Svelte virgins then
stout ladies now,
middle aged or blue haired,
coupled countless times,
with children of their own
or grandchildren
next in line to scream
for some aphrodisiac celebrity,
some brimming with disappointments,
others quite content,
some sadly disaffected,
others romantics still
but all knowing now that life is,
if you'll pardon the expression,
no bowl of cherries.

STILL DELIGHTING

WATERMELON DAYS

Here I am, a graybeard, eating watermelon
and remembering those summers
when I could count my age in single digits,
summers at the lake
where the cousins would assemble for dinner
around my grandmother's large table.
Though there's plenty of melon in the fridge
I find myself cutting close to the rind
as I did in those days,
and there I am,
still that boy at seventy-three,
at the table with the Tiffany lamp overhead
or descending the hill to the lake,
its water smooth and green
lapping softly on the shore
and the sound of mourning doves in counterpoint.

STILL DELIGHTING IN SNOW

I still delight in snow
some seventy years after I first did.
Though my body now is tentative,
I still take pleasure
in that world of whiteness
just as I did when I resided
in a frame so small
I can no longer remember how it felt.
I sense boy-feelings of decades ago,
flakes on my lashes,
against my skin,
the bracing scent,
the compact blizzard
as I tumbled from my sled,
a scattering of cold powder
turning my eyebrows white—
as now do other causes—
my clothes encrusted,
the wetness soaking through,
the warm kitchen
where I disrobed
("Get out of those wet clothes!"
my mother said)
fading
into the one where I sit now
tapping out this poem.

A World That Was

As I turn on the radio
this Saturday afternoon
opera swells out
from where I left the dial
and I'm transmitted back
more than half the century
to those peaceful prewar days
when I had no intimation
of what the future held,
and our radio
with its gothic wooden case
was tuned to the Met
in the living room
surrounded by birch and magnolia trees
and the long, smooth slope of the lawn.

I associated opera then
with dull times
when I was house-bound
and would restlessly quarter
that thicket of sound
chafing for something to do.
For years after
I never cared much for opera,
but it sings to me now
of a world that was
in a child's hopeful eyes.

LISTENING TO RAVEL

Playing a recording
of Ravel piano works
as I do paperwork,
I only half listen,
but my mind is wafted by the music
like a sailboat in a shifting breeze,
as if the sky were summer blue
tufted with clouds,
and I were somewhere off the coast
of Normandy, or inland perhaps
in a sparsely furnished room,
sunlight falling through arched glass doors.

SILVER IS THE COLOR
OF MY TRUE LOVE'S HAIR

as if some cunning craftsman
had spun metal
into silken thread.
It was chestnut brown when we met.
Her skin, all smooth then,
has begun to show fine webs
and is slack under her once firm chin.
But, when I look on her, I think
this is the girl I wed
and feel the need to kiss her cheek
or if she's bent over some task,
the nape of her neck
or if she's sitting with the hem of her dress
resting on her thighs,
to reach out and touch her knee.

SUGAR AND SPICE

"My darling boy," says my wife.
"Your septuagenarian boy," say I.
Fact is I feel more boy than seventy some.
But it's rather, I suppose,
my wife adoring that imaginary boy
of photos from the family album.
And for my part I love the girl
once blond and looking shy
and imagine her
laughing with her friends
the way girls do
more readily than boys,
and see her sitting knobby kneed
behind her school desk
knowing the answer
but too reticent to raise her hand.
I see her now
inside this gray-haired woman
who speaks her mind.

I FEEL YOUR HEARTBEAT

I feel your heartbeat
even though we're not touching
when we see each other and smile
after I've been away.

I feel your heartbeat
even though you're not at home
when I come upon
the sentimental gift I gave you
sitting on your pillow.

I feel your heartbeat
when I call you at your office
just to say hello.

I feel your heartbeat
and mine scats
in syncopated rhythm
round your metronome.

SILLY MAN

I was a serious boy
and most of my life
rarely indulged in silliness.
Oh, I was prone to the inadvertent kind,
slips I chastised myself for,
causing me to avoid the deliberate sort all the more.
Then I married a woman who liked my jokes
and gradually I extended them
into a bit of clowning.
She laughed and I clowned some more
and again she laughed.
I was energized,
like a dog walking on its hind legs
encouraged by applause,
and the more my audience of one applauded
the more I two-footed it,
progressing to splits and fast buck-and-wings.
Now I even clown in public, sometimes,
and when I do, publicly or privately,
I feel lighter for it.
At this rate I'll end up floating away
like a helium-filled balloon.

SURROUNDED BY THE UNIVERSE

In these early morning hours
in this room
it begins
stretching outward
from the circle of lamplight on my desk
to the leaf-dappled streetlight across the way
to the moon's chalky mirror
to the distant incandescence of the stars,
from the scratch of my pen
to the scrapings of insects in surrounding fields
to the faint but ceaseless aura of traffic sounds
through the intermittent silences of space
to the obliterating but unheard stellar roar,
and so to the dead-quiet edges of this universe
where starlight thins to blackness,
from the small circle of lamplight
on my desk.

PLAY JOLLY MUSIC AT MY FUNERAL

I've taken in recent years to thinking about my funeral
and have decided to make one paramount request:
play jolly music at that ritual.
What good does it do to heap on dirges?
I won't be there to be gratified by the grieving
and if I could tune in
I'd be happier to see those present have some relief.
Jelly Roll would be nice.
Joplin would be fine.
Something by Fats Waller would certainly do.
Those early jazzmen knew what they were up to
when they set about making funeral marches swing.
So swing me away, please, with a rousing tune.

LAST WORDS

I'm ready to cross the river now
on this rickety raft of bones
in this bag of sagging skin.
Let me swim.
All my life I've swum,
beginning in the womb.
Now is no time
to start riding in boats.

ABOUT THE AUTHOR

Dick Greene, a retired international development program planner and manager, first became interested in poetry at age eight when his parents bought him a set of children's books, one of which was a volume of poetry. Among the poems in that volume was Burns' "To a Mouse," which captivated him then, as it does still. Introduced to Longfellow's *Evangeline* in eighth grade, he was inspired by its majestic opening lines to try his hand at writing poetry.

Soon after beginning his freshman year in college, he showed a sample of his work to a young lady in one of his classes, who declared it trite—his poem rhymed at a time when modernism was in the ascendant—and he stopped writing poetry for two years. Then in his junior year he encountered Henry Rago, editor of *Poetry,* who taught the section of a humanities course to which he'd been assigned. He began poetizing again.

After college Dick attended law school and continued writing poems, but wrote few then or afterwards when he served in the army for two years and subsequently entered upon his 38-year international development career. Toward the end of that career, he began to write poetry again, enjoying the support and editorial wisdom of his wife, Celeste, and continued to write even more intensively after retiring, first to New Jersey and more recently to Massachusetts. He currently lives in Northampton.

Dick has had little interest in publishing his work in journals, preferring instead to email a weekly poem to family, friends and acquaintances, and to correspond with the many readers who send him their reactions.

An Invitation

Readers of this book who wish to receive the author's Poem of the Week should send their names and addresses to greeneplace@gmail. com. Comments on this book and individual poems in it are also welcome and may be sent to the same address. In addition, readers are invited to visit Dick's website, www.greenepage.net, where his weekly poems and other writings are posted.

This book is set in Garamond Premier Pro, which originated in 1988 when type-designer Robert Slimbach visited the Plantin-Moretus Museum in Antwerp, Belgium, to study its collection of Claude Garamond's metal punches and typefaces. During the mid-1500's, Garamond—a Parisian punch-cutter—produced a refined array of book types that combined an unprecedented degree of balance and elegance, for centuries standing as the pinnacle of beauty and practicality in type-founding. Slimbach has created an entirely new interpretation based on Garamond's designs and on comparable italics cut by Robert Granjon, Garamond's contemporary.

To order additional copies of this book
or other Antrim House titles, contact the publisher at

Antrim House
21 Goodrich Rd., Simsbury, CT 06070
860.217.0023, AntrimHouse@comcast.net
or the house website (www.AntrimHouseBooks.com).

•

On the house website
are sample poems, upcoming events,
and a "seminar room" featuring supplemental notes,
reviews, images, poems, discussion topics,
and writing suggestions offered by
Antrim House poets.